**Positive and Practical Advice
to Help You Live Life to the Full**

THE POWER OF
YES
—

ABBIE HEADON

ilex

CONTENTS

THE POWER OF

YES

_

An Hachette UK Company
www.hachette.co.uk

First published in Great Britain in 2018
by Ilex, a division of
Octopus Publishing Group Ltd
Carmelite House
50 Victoria Embankment
London EC4Y 0DZ
www.octopusbooks.co.uk

Distributed in the US by
Hachette Book Group
1290 Avenue of the Americas
4th and 5th Floors
New York, NY 10104

Distributed in Canada by
Canadian Manda Group
664 Annette St.
Toronto, Ontario, Canada M6S 2C8

Publisher: Roly Allen
Editorial Director: Helen Rochester
Commissioning Editor: Zara Anvari
Managing Editor:
Frank Gallaugher
Editor: Jenny Dye
Publishing Assistant:
Stephanie Hetherington
Art Director: Julie Weir
Designer: Ben Gardiner
Production Manager: Caroline Alberti

ISBN 978-1-78157-600-7

A CIP catalogue record for this book
is available from the British Library.

Printed and bound in China

10 9 8 7 6 5 4 3 2 1

Picture credits:
Shutterstock: AlexHliv – page 31,
Christine Schmidt – page 46 and
repeat, Creativika Graphics – page 5
and repeat, Creators Club – page 14
and repeat, Creators Club – page 24
and repeat, Curly Roo – page 22 and
repeat, DistanceO – cover, Dolvalol –
page 36, Fay Francevna – page 13
and repeat, liskus – page 30 and
repeat, liskus – page 32 and repeat,
Perfect Vectors – page 40 and repeat,
Samolevsky – page 16 and repeat,
Waranon – page 37, yayha – pages 28
and 29.

INTRODUCTION
SAY HELLO TO YES!

Welcome to *The Power of YES* – it's great to have you here. We're going to look at how to bring as much joy and achievement as possible to every day. Because you get so much more out of life when you approach it with a 'yes'!

In these pages, you'll discover what puts the spark into life and what helps us achieve our goals. Of course, everybody has moments of self-doubt and fluctuating amounts of 'yes-ness' in their life, myself included. That's why I've enjoyed writing about positivity in all its forms – because I know how great and energised I feel when I'm bursting with it, and I've spent a *lot* of time thinking about what the magic ingredients are that make life more fulfilling and satisfying.

I've divided the book into thematic chapters, each focusing on a different part of life. We'll start by **checking in** with how we're feeling right now and then dive in deep to look at our **dreams** and ambitions. We'll step out into the big wide world with a chapter on **exploring**, expand our minds with a focus on **learning** and welcome the working week with a section on **careers**. We'll look at how to build empowering **relationships** with friends, family members and partners, and then focus in on **loving ourselves**. Then it's time to look at how to make our **home** the perfect place to relax, before snuggling down with the best ways to **rest**. Finally, refreshed and full of energy, we'll head out and start **changing the world**.

Every chapter contains three **Yes Labs**, giving you concrete ideas on how to bring more 'yes' into your life, along with tips to help you **Tune Out the Critics** – both internal and external. **A Story of Yes** presents amazing people who've achieved great things just by listening to their inner 'yes', to inspire you to have faith in yours, and at the end of each chapter, **Yes, But...** looks at how we can overcome obstacles we might face and make sure our 'yeses' work for us.

Join me on an adventure into positivity, and discover the power of YES.

CHECK-IN
BEFORE WE BEGIN...

Let's start by taking a look at where you are right now. Decide how true each of the statements in the table are for you, and tick the box that matches how you feel.

In some areas you might feel confident and strong, while for others you may wish things could be different. That's what this book is here for: we're going to look at each of these subjects in turn, giving you tips to help you move your ticks closer to the 'Always' column.

Every journey starts with a single step ... so let's begin, together. You'll be amazed how far you can go once you discover your inner 'yes'.

I believe I can achieve my dreams

I enjoy exploring the world around me

My life gives me opportunities to learn new things

My career is moving forward

My relationships are satisfying

I am happy with who I am and how I look

My home makes me feel at home

After resting, I feel refreshed and ready for anything

I believe I can change the world

NEVER	NOT OFTEN	SOMETIMES	OFTEN	ALWAYS

1

SAY YES TO DREAMING BIG

Remember when you were a child, pretending to be a princess, an explorer, a pop star? Suddenly you *became* that person. The world was a playground: the space under your dining table could be a cave, and the carpet around your bed could be a sea full of ravenous sharks. Your imagination permitted you to do anything, and *be* anything, without fear or second-guessing.

As we get older, we tend to lose some of this childhood freedom. We develop fixed ideas and beliefs about ourselves, our personalities and our jobs, and we think less about all those other opportunities that are out there waiting for us.

But the truth is that the rules we set for ourselves can be broken. Whatever your current job is and whatever you tell yourself about your abilities, you have the power to change things, both in your life and in the wider world. In this chapter we're going to reawaken the super-imaginative, creative you, and connect you with your greatest power – the power to dream and to make those dreams a reality.

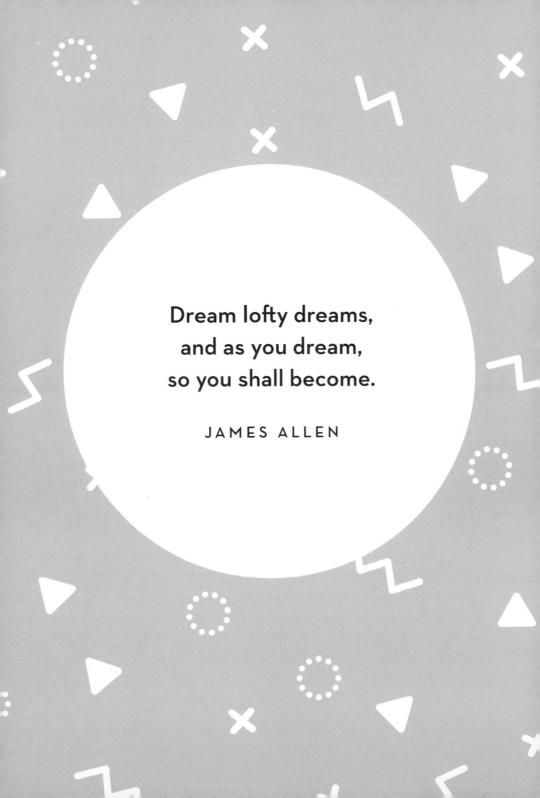

Dream lofty dreams,
and as you dream,
so you shall become.

JAMES ALLEN

YES LAB

FIND YOUR GOALS

———

We all have huge reserves of untapped power and potential – all we need to do is identify a goal and then start moving towards it. So let's start.

Think about the areas of your life that are most important to you. These could include your work, your love life, your creative side – it's up to you. Copy the template below, and use it to help you lay out your thoughts.

Now, think about how you'd like to change and develop in relation to each area. Maybe you like your job but it doesn't stretch you, or you want to make one of the key relationships in your life more positive and fulfilling.

For the next stage, focus in on each goal, and ask yourself what you'll need to achieve it. You might choose some additional training to help you get to the next level of your career, or perhaps you need to spend more time with the person you want to improve your connection with. One or two ideas will be enough to get you started.

Finally, write down how you'll know when you've reached your goal. This will give you something very real and solid to aim for – and you'll know when you've got there.

Topic	
I want to...	
Here's what I'll need to achieve this	
Achieving my goal will look like this	

YES LAB

DARE TO FAIL

———

One of the things that holds us back from trying to achieve our dreams is the fear of failure. And that's not unreasonable – when a new venture doesn't work, it can leave us feeling discouraged. This toolkit will help you learn how to cope with failure and see its plus sides.

RESILIENCE HELPS: We all face setbacks, and the people who succeed are often those who stick at it when times get tough. Notice how you cope with everyday disasters like missing your bus. Do you fall apart or look for a plan B? Resilience is an incredibly valuable trait to develop, and practising it in your daily life will help you when you need it for your bigger projects.

YOU DON'T HAVE TO BE PERFECT: It's all very well wanting to be the best at everything you do, but it's not very realistic. If you wait to be perfect at something before you give it a proper go, you might be waiting for ever. Allow 'good enough' to be your entry point to a new project and you'll be amazed at what you can do.

REFRAME THE NARRATIVE: A failure could be the end of the road for your dream, a sign that you were being overambitious. OR ... a failure could be a learning opportunity, showing you how to fine-tune your original model before you start again. We all have the choice to let failure stop us or turn it into something that helps us achieve success in the long run.

TUNE OUT THE CRITICS

"If it goes wrong, it will be a total disaster."

The name for this thought process is 'catastrophising', and like perfectionism, it doesn't do us any good. We evolved to be risk-averse, but nowadays the risks we face are usually less deadly than being eaten by a sabre-toothed tiger or falling off a cliff. Ask yourself: what's the worst that could happen? Create a mental picture of yourself coping with it – and then get on with following your dream.

"You're not the kind of person who..."

Anyone who is keen to tell you all about your limitations is in fact telling you far more about their own, so give this kind of negativity the amount of time it deserves: none at all. Someone with constructive advice to give will frame it in an encouraging way to guide you forward on your path. A true friend won't fill your life with can'ts.

Ever tried. Ever failed. No matter. Try again. Fail again. Fail better.

SAMUEL BECKETT

A STORY OF YES
J. K. ROWLING

In 1990, during a delayed train journey, J. K. Rowling came up with a story about a boy named Harry Potter who goes to a wizardry school. It's now one of the best-selling books of all time, but back then it was an idea, just waiting to be conjured into being. During the following five years, Rowling lost her mother to multiple sclerosis, separated from her husband and suffered from clinical depression, but despite all these setbacks, she kept writing.

When she finished the book, Rowling received 12 rejections before a publisher agreed to take it on. Since her first title was published in 1997, over 500 million Harry Potter books have been sold and the story has triumphed on stage and screen. Rowling advocates for charities and has started her own, Lumos, which helps children in orphanages and is named after the light-giving spell in her books.

While J. K. Rowling's story is one of remarkable success, what it demonstrates is that if you keep going when times are hard, and never give up, eventually you can make something wonderful happen. So never stop believing in magic – the magic of your positive attitude.

The world is full of
wonderful things
you haven't seen
yet. Don't ever give
up on the chance
of seeing them.

J. K. ROWLING

YES LAB

AND NOW FOR SOMETHING COMPLETELY DIFFERENT

———

If you're not sure exactly what your goal is, or what the 'yes' is that you're looking for, step outside your usual routine and try sparking your ideas and dreams in a new way.

TRY SOMETHING DIFFERENT FOR 30 DAYS:

Set yourself the challenge of doing something new each month. You could start hobbies such as baking or crafting, or set good habits in motion such as getting eight hours of sleep a night. Thirty days is just enough time to immerse yourself your chosen activity – but it also gives you the chance to experiment with something else the next month. Constantly pushing yourself to try different things will remind you of that view of the world you had as a child, when everything you experienced was fresh and exciting, and will open up your mind to new possibilities.

GO SOMEWHERE NEW: The same places are often the source of the same kinds of ideas. But you don't have to go very far to find inspiration – just take a different route to work or head out in a new direction on your lunch break. Philosophers have known for centuries that being around trees and plants is good for the spirit, so green surroundings are also great places to stimulate your creativity. Whether you're in a different neighbourhood, a city park or an untamed wilderness, look out for the new directions your mind starts travelling in – and enjoy the journey.

The future belongs to
those who believe in the
beauty of their dreams.

ELEANOR ROOSEVELT

YES, BUT...

Your dreams will change throughout your life, and so will your levels of confidence and energy in achieving them. Pretty much nothing in life that's worthwhile is easy, and not everything you try will be a success. But by keeping an open mind, trusting in yourself, making small steps forward and never punishing yourself when you slip back, you'll have the best chance of making your dreams become real. Just keep working towards your goals – even on those days when everything seems against you.

2

SAY YES TO EXPLORING

Now that we've set our dreams into motion, it's time to look beyond the shores of our own existence. Travel doesn't have to be a year-long, bank-breaking voyage: what's important is a spirit of adventure. In this chapter, we'll look at three ways of saying 'yes' to exploration, through microadventures, quests and trips into the unknown. Here are just some of the benefits of stamping a 'yes' on your passport.

Understand other cultures:
When you travel, you'll come across traditions, styles of dress, types of food and lots of other things that are new to you. Getting to know another culture more deeply will open you up to new ways of thinking.

Develop resourcefulness:
'Things go wrong' is one of the universal laws of travelling – and when they do, you'll have no choice but to make the best of the situation. These moments of stress will help you find your inner strength.

Understand yourself better:
When you put yourself in a strange
new situation, your emotions and
reactions will be different to those you
experience in everyday life, and you'll
discover more about what makes
you tick as a person.

**Discover what links
us all together:**
The more you travel, the easier
it is to see that beneath our
superficial differences, everyone
shares a common humanity, faces
the same struggles and celebrates
the same victories. This is perhaps
the best 'yes' that travel offers us.

YES LAB

FIND TIME FOR A
MICROADVENTURE

———

The term 'microadventure' was coined by Alastair Humphreys, a man with plenty of macroadventures under his belt, such as cycling around the world.

A microadventure is a short, simple, cheap adventure that you can do as part of your normal life – you don't even have to camp out all night. Once you start using your imagination, there are lots of activities you could try in your free time that would get your adventuring juices flowing...

TRAVEL TO A RANDOM
POINT ON THE MAP

HAVE A CAMPFIRE
ON THE BEACH

GO ON A
NIGHT WALK

FOLLOW A
HISTORIC PATH

HIRE A
CANAL BOAT

GET OFF YOUR TRAIN AT
A NEW STOP, AND FIND
YOUR WAY HOME

GO FISHING –
AND THEN EAT
YOUR CATCH
FOR DINNER

YES LAB

START OUT
ON A QUEST

———

Whether you're close to home or on the other side of the world, one way to become a true explorer is to set out on a quest. When you're searching for an X that marks the spot, you'll be more observant and engaged with your surroundings than if you were simply passing through.

GET THE GEOCACHING HABIT: Set out on an outdoor expedition and make connections with fellow questers by joining the online geocaching community. You'll find locations of 'caches' near and far, each one containing a logbook and possibly some small treasures for you to enjoy or swap.

EXPLORE HISTORY AND LEGEND: Find out which historical or mythical characters are associated with the area you're visiting. With a little research, you could follow the footsteps of a Roman centurion or visit the cave where a legendary dragon once lived. Finding the stories beneath your feet will make your experience richer.

TEST YOURSELF WITH A TREASURE HUNT: Available online or from tourist offices, these trails offer a series of clues to unpick, and you'll learn lots about the place you're exploring as you travel. You could even create your own treasure hunt for a group of friends and put each other's skills to the test.

A STORY OF YES
FELICITY ASTON

After finishing her university studies, Felicity Aston went to Antarctica in 2000 to work for the British Antarctic Survey as a meteorologist, monitoring climate and the ozone layer. Aged just 23, she accepted the challenge of living in the coldest and most remote part of the planet for two and a half years, and ever since then she has been a committed adventurer and explorer.

In 2009, Felicity led an expedition of seven women from six British Commonwealth nations on a journey to the South Pole; it was the largest and most international team of women ever to achieve this goal. Some of the women on the trip had never seen snow before joining the expedition, and along the way, they experienced hardships together and formed strong bonds.

Felicity has continued to share her knowledge and love of adventure with countless travellers, and has been awarded the Queen's Polar Medal and an MBE for her services to polar exploration. Her story shows that when we say 'yes' to adventure, we can push ourselves beyond our normal limits and end up sharing our achievements with many more people.

It gave people the courage to follow their dreams and I felt really proud of that.

FELICITY ASTON
ON HER GROUP EXPEDITION
TO THE SOUTH POLE

YES LAB

GET OUTSIDE YOUR COMFORT ZONE

———

You've probably noticed this already, but it's worth saying all the same: life doesn't always go exactly the way we plan. One way of preparing yourself for life's ups and downs is to willingly put yourself in situations that stretch you a little.

Here's a selection of things you might like to try that will take you beyond your comfort zone. Why not roll a dice and see where fortune leads you?

 Travel alone, setting your own timetable and making all your own rules.

 Sleep somewhere unusual, whether it's a yurt, a dormitory or a treehouse.

 Eat food you've never had before, such as kimchi, sashimi or witchetty grubs.

 Experience a different climate, from the snowy tundra to the equatorial rainforest.

 Feel the adrenaline rush of crossing a rope bridge, scuba diving or taking to the skies on a hang-glider.

 Go engine-free by travelling under your own steam, on foot, by bicycle or in a kayak.

TUNE OUT
THE CRITICS

"What if I get there and I don't like the food, or there are spiders...?"

It's always a risk going somewhere new: for every wonderful experience you're likely to encounter an inconvenience of some kind. But that's all part of the challenge of travelling. You can take away a lot of the fear of the unknown by researching your destination and making sure you've got everything you'll need. A first-aid kit is an essential, and a comfortable pillow will help you bring the feeling of home wherever you go.

*"But I don't speak the language –
I'll never cope!"*

Learning some key phrases and words before you set off will help you feel prepared – and don't let lack of fluency be an obstacle. It's amazing how far you can get with goodwill, a phrase book and a lot of gestures. People are much more willing to communicate than you'd imagine, and finding ways to express yourself will put your creativity to the test (and provide some excellent anecdotes along the way).

All you need is the plan, the road map and the courage to press on to your destination.

EARL NIGHTINGALE

One's destination is never
a place but rather a new
way of looking at things.

HENRY MILLER

YES, BUT...

Travel to exotic, beautiful locations is one of those things that everyone on social media seems to be doing; in reality we all have a finite amount of time and money, not to mention energy. But these limitations shouldn't stop us. Sometimes thinking 'big' means we forget to make the most of what's on our doorstep. It's not about how far you travel, or how often – all of us can seize the spirit of adventure when the time is right, whether we're heading out on an afternoon walk, a weekend expedition or a once-in-a-lifetime trip to a new continent. The world really is your oyster – and it's out there waiting for you to discover it.

3

SAY YES TO
LEARNING

Keeping your mind active and stimulated will improve your quality of life and may even benefit your health. Through acquiring knowledge and gaining new skills, you can significantly improve your well-being and happiness. Learning happens inside and outside classrooms, when we talk to friends, watch television, read and try new things. And it has lots of incredible benefits.

INCREASE EMPATHY:
Study an area outside your experience to broaden your view of the world. Your brain will get valuable practice in thinking outside its usual lines, helping you relate to others with different backgrounds and opinions.

DEVELOP YOUR CAREER:
You could gain a new skill towards a promotion or even a complete career change, or focus on something to help you excel in your current role.

THINK CRITICALLY:
Working to understand new systems and structures improves your ability to question the status quo, and may even lead you to start changing the world around you for the better.

IMPROVE CREATIVITY:
From glass-blowing and banjo-making to tap dancing and Russian conversation, you could learn literally anything – and each subject will influence your creative side in exciting new ways.

HEALTH BOOST:
Learning can increase people's sense of mental well-being, and some researchers believe that education throughout life helps keep our brains young and active.

REDUCE ANXIETY:
When your mind is completely engrossed by a challenging task that demands your full attention, you can find yourself in a 'flow' state, where your deep focus allows all your usual worries to fade away.

YES LAB

RELIGHT YOUR (LEARNING) FIRE

———

We'll begin by helping you decide what to study, and how to start your learning journey.

STEP 1: First, think about what you want to learn. Take a big blank piece of paper and fill it with your ideas. Give your imagination free rein and let all your thoughts spill onto the page, however wacky.

STEP 2: Now it's time to choose which idea to follow up first. Maybe there's one clear winner – something you've always wanted to do. If you can't decide, you could leave it to chance, randomly selecting by rolling a dice. Alternatively, pick one by considering which course would help you with your wider goals, such as career development or fitness.

STEP 3: Research time! Find out where the subject is taught and think about what setting you would prefer. Do you want to join a group class or have one-to-one lessons? Can you take a course online?

STEP 4: All you need to do now is enrol and get ready for your first session. If you have a friend who would like to learn with you, so much the better. Having a study buddy will help you stick with the course, and you'll be able to bounce ideas off each other too.

YES LAB

ASK QUESTIONS

———

Push beyond "how are you?" and get to know your colleagues, friends and family better. Ask open questions about what they enjoy, how they really feel and what they want. Listen and take the time to absorb what they have to say.

Everyone is unique and brings different questions to the table, so to gain new angles on a subject, why not set up an informal study group? Arrange a time to regularly meet up with a few friends who share a common interest, such as books, films, art or nature. It doesn't have to be too structured, and you don't need to be experts. If you're going to talk about a popular book or film, you can often download discussion questions to guide you, or you might like to set your own. You could also write your questions and opinions on pieces of card and then pull them out of a hat in a random order to discuss them – this is a great way to encourage discussion without feeling that the spotlight is on you.

TUNE OUT
THE CRITICS

"Ha! You – learning French! Ooh la la!"

The sad truth is that sometimes, when we show signs of growth and change, other people around us can feel threatened, because they are afraid they're getting left behind. When this happens, the best thing to do is take a breath and acknowledge that yes, you are studying something new. Stay calm, quiet and friendly, and then allow the conversation to move on. Your critics will run out of steam pretty quickly, and your mind will be free to focus on more important things, such as the new learning adventure you've embarked upon.

"I was rubbish at school."

School-related anxiety is shared by most of us – after all, we've all had some kind of horribly embarrassing experience in our school days, and nobody likes getting back an exercise covered in red ink. Learning as an adult is completely different. You're likely to be in a much smaller group, with supportive classmates and a relaxed and friendly teacher. And it's no longer compulsory: you've chosen a subject because you're passionate about it. Give yourself a chance to feel the joy of learning again – you won't regret it.

What you do today can improve all your tomorrows.

RALPH MARSTON

A STORY OF YES
MALALA YOUSAFZAI

Malala Yousafzai, born in the Swat Valley in Pakistan in 1997, became a prominent blogger and campaigner for the right of girls to be educated. In 2012, she was shot in the head at point-blank range by a Taliban gunman. His aim was to silence her, but he didn't succeed: after a painful recovery process, Malala returned to her campaigning with more vigour than ever, and with even more support and admiration from the global community.

In 2014, Malala was awarded the Nobel Peace Prize, becoming the youngest ever Nobel laureate, and in the autumn of 2017 she started studying at the University of Oxford. Her organisation, the Malala Fund, operates in areas where girls are less likely to receive secondary education, continuing her courageous work.

What Malala went through is far more extreme than most of us will ever experience, but her bravery, dignity and passion for education can inspire us all.

There is no greater weapon than knowledge and no greater source of knowledge than the written word.

MALALA YOUSAFZAI

YES LAB

THE KNOWLEDGE
EXCHANGE

———

It may sound surprising, but one of the best ways to learn is to teach. This is because teaching requires us to take our knowledge and use it actively: it's not just sitting there quietly in a drawer at the back of our brains, but being used, questioned and extended in discussion with somebody who wants to understand it as well as we do.

Even if you're not a trained teacher, you can practise teaching and gain a new skill at the same time by setting up a teaching exchange. Either through your circle of friends or a local message board, find somebody who has a skill they can teach you in return for something you can teach them. The classic teaching exchange is with languages. You meet and spend half the time speaking in your language and half the time in the other person's language – but you can think outside the box and swap guitar lessons for car maintenance, or flower arranging for spreadsheet-formula wizardry.

As well as being an opportunity to learn something new, sharing your knowledge will help you value yourself and understand just how much you have to give. And once you've realised that, there will be no stopping you on your positivity journey.

The important
thing is not to
stop questioning.

ALBERT EINSTEIN

YES, BUT...

We all lead busy lives, and it can be hard to find the time and energy for learning, especially if it's more of a 'fun' project than something you need right now in your life. If you find your other commitments – or your need to spend an evening on the sofa – getting in the way, don't beat yourself up: it's OK to miss a class, or even to decide that a course isn't right for you. But here are two things that might help you stick with your plans: first, take a step back and remind yourself what your original motivation was – focusing on a goal will help you keep going; second, make your learning part of a regular routine, rather than something you slot in at irregular moments – if you know that you study Spanish every Tuesday at 7pm, you'll be much less likely to put it off till mañana.

SAY YES TO YOUR CAREER

4

Approaching your career with a 'yes' frame of mind will help you achieve success. When we think about our work, negative phrases can often come to the surface: *it's too late to retrain, you're too old to change career* and so on. The truth is that it's never too late to breathe new life into your career – or make a break and try something completely different.

If you're feeling stuck and in need of a change, ask yourself honestly where you'd rather be and what you'd rather be doing. Once you can see your goal in your imagination, think about how you can get there. It may not be easy, but it's almost certainly possible.

You'll find ideas and techniques in this chapter that will help you make the most of the time you spend at work and expand your career horizons.

Find out what you like doing
best and get someone
to pay you for it.

KATHARINE WHITEHORN

YES LAB

DEAL WITH DISTRACTIONS

———

For many of us, the biggest obstacle to our progress at work is distraction. Here are some tips to help you kick the D-word into the long grass.

START WITH AN ACTIVE TASK: It can be tempting to check your emails first thing, but if you start by reacting to other people's needs, you're deprioritising your own goals before your first cup of coffee has even cooled down. You'll achieve more if you put your own tasks first and *then* deal with your inbox.

PLAY TO YOUR BODY CLOCK'S STRENGTHS: Some of us get most done in the morning, while others come into their own later in the day. If you're not sure when your best times are, keep a diary for a few days, marking your energy ebbs and flows. Schedule your most concentrated work into your most productive time slots.

REMOVE DISTRACTIONS: Place any non-essential gadgets out of sight (a drawer or a bag is ideal). When you aren't constantly being made aware of all the fascinating things happening online, you'll be able to get on with making things happen in your work life instead.

GIVE YOURSELF REWARDS: When you feel the pull of a distraction, remind yourself of something you've stored up for the end of this working period. It could be a cup of tea or simply the glorious satisfaction of pressing 'send' on that report you've been working on for weeks.

YES LAB

BUILD YOUR OWN NETWORK

———

Networking is a very useful skill to learn: you could find a new client, learn about an innovation to use in your department or even chat your way into a new job. You have nothing to lose and everything to gain.

INTERNAL NETWORKING: Make the most of all the connections available to you in your own workplace. You could arrange to have lunch with a more senior colleague who could act as a mentor, or meet up with an equal from another department to learn about a different area of your industry. The more you reach beyond your usual contacts and look at the bigger picture, the more doors you'll be able to open.

INDUSTRY NETWORKING: With a little bit of research, you can find a variety of events where people in your industry come together, from official conferences to informal pub meetups. Try reaching out on Twitter beforehand to make a link that you can follow up in person on the night. Putting yourself out there is a great way to find new opportunities.

SUPPORT CIRCLE: Organise a monthly session with your friends where your mission is to discuss each other's work worries and successes, brainstorm solutions and suggest interesting new directions. It can be hard standing up for our own dreams, but it's in the nature of friendship that we champion each other's.

TUNE OUT
THE CRITICS

*"Networking is
a waste of time."*

The important thing to remember is that people
employ people. Networking is only unproductive
if we don't follow up on the contacts we've made,
so make sure you keep in touch and prepare to be
surprised by new opportunities.

> *"But I hate networking events –
> I never know what to say."*
>
> The easiest way to engage someone is to offer to help them.
> By giving before you ask for something in return, the person
> you're reaching out to will be invested in you. If you can't find
> the courage to talk to the CEO, speak to someone you think
> is making tracks to becoming a key influencer in the future.
> If nothing else, you'll have a very interesting discussion.

The way of the world is meeting people through other people.

ROBERT KERRIGAN

A STORY OF YES
NATE MARTIN

Escape rooms, locked spaces where groups of friends works together to solve fiendish clues, are now a popular form of entertainment. In 2013, escape rooms were well known in Europe and Asia, but not in the USA. Nate Martin, a former software engineer at Microsoft and Electronic Arts, saw an opportunity and grabbed it with both hands. He and his business partner Lindsay Morse founded Puzzle Break with an initial investment of just $7,000 of Nate's own money. Their risk paid off: very soon the venture became a word-of-mouth success, earning a revenue of over $1 million in 2016. As well as running centres in various locations across the USA, Nate established escape rooms in a fleet of cruise ships, making his operation truly global.

And the moral of the story? If you see an opportunity, trust your instincts and prepare to plunge into a new and exciting experience. If you have the will to succeed, you'll be amazed at just how far your positive attitude can take you in your career just as in the rest of your life.

There's no reason why you can't start small and put your toes in the water and just do it.

NATE MARTIN

YES LAB

NEGOTIATE YOUR
WAY TO SUCCESS

———

Negotiating isn't just the preserve of business magnates: actually, it's something we all do, whether we're bargaining on behalf of the organisation we work for or asking for a pay rise. These tips will help you reach a successful result and find a mutual 'yes' in your next negotiation.

STAY CALM: Remind yourself that this is a conversation between equals – you both have something to offer and you both deserve to be heard. Focus on a positive outcome and take a few deep breaths.

LOOK FOR A WIN-WIN: If you're asking for something, give evidence to support your case. Then work for a result that brings advantages to you both – you'll each leave the conversation feeling like winners.

PREPARE TO COMPROMISE: Go into the conversation with a plan B for other positive outcomes. If you can't have a raise right now, for example, you could agree on a date for a reassessment of the situation, or ask for a training course or a change of job title.

KEEP THE CONVERSATION GOING: Finally, if you don't get what you want this time, don't lose heart: end the discussion on a friendly note and agree to return to the subject at a later date. Persistence and positivity will get you a long way.

It is never too late
to be what you
might have been.

GEORGE ELIOT

YES, BUT...

Our career paths usually involve a balance of hopes and needs, and it's not always possible to land that dream job. And of course, sometimes the only important thing is to have *any* kind of a job. Realise that wherever you are at the moment, you have the power to make your career more rewarding. This could involve finding ways to get more fulfilment out of your current job, working towards a promotion, or gaining experience that would help you move into a completely different role. Acknowledge what you're good at, and look for opportunities that will help you grow – and if you're able to engage the power of your support network, this will give you the best chance of building a career that you enjoy and that also gets the bills paid.

5

SAY YES TO GREAT RELATIONSHIPS

Pretty much everything we do in life is influenced by our relationships – we exist in a network of interlocking connections, each of us playing multiple roles in different people's lives at the same time. Human connections bring us joy and energy, and it has been shown that loneliness is as bad for your health as a chronic medical condition.

However, as we all know, relationships can also bring many challenges, and it can be extremely difficult to think about them calmly, as they engage our most basic emotions of desire, jealousy and fear of rejection. But what we can do is dedicate time to our relationships and practise strategies that will help them flourish. In this chapter, we'll focus on what makes a supportive friendship, how to keep relationships fresh and how to compromise – leaving you free to make your connections even stronger.

One does not fall 'in' or 'out' of love. One grows in love.

LEO BUSCAGLIA

YES LAB

GOOD FRIENDS WANT YOU TO GROW

———

The mutual desire to see each other succeed is an important foundation of a good friendship.

We receive a lot of training in competitive thinking when we're young, with our siblings and schoolmates. There's always a game to be won or lost, a quiz to come first or last in, an exam to pass or fail. But competitive thinking doesn't get us very far in our personal lives, and sometimes we need to remind ourselves to celebrate others' achievements.

Try these ideas, and watch your relationships grow deeper as a result.

- SUPPORT EACH OTHER'S AMBITIONS

- PRAISE EACH OTHER'S SUCCESSES

- ENCOURAGE EACH OTHER TO AIM HIGH

- SEE SUCCESSFUL PEOPLE AS POTENTIAL ALLIES, NOT RIVALS

- SHARE RESOURCES, TIPS AND KNOWLEDGE WITH EACH OTHER

YES LAB

DON'T GET INTO
THE GROOVE

——

With all the other pressures of life, sometimes we can allow our friendships and romantic relationships to get a bit samey, a bit stuck in a rut. We can avoid losing the spark by following a few simple steps.

BE SPONTANEOUS: Remember when you first met your partner or a close friend? You had no backstory, no fixed expectations of what they were like. Bring back some of that initial magic by suggesting new ideas and activities that you can do together.

BE YOURSELF: We have to pretend to be more grown-up and sorted out than we actually are quite a lot of the time. When you're with your loved ones, it's time to let your guard down and express your real hopes and fears.

TALK TO EACH OTHER: We have a million ways of connecting now, with emails, tweets and many more options besides. But there's nothing to beat an actual conversation. An "I'm fine" on screen might turn out to be "I'm not actually fine at all" when you phone – and those conversations are the ones our close relationships are there for.

KEEP IT REAL: There might be something you want to change about your relationship – for example, maybe you're not communicating enough, or one of you is always cancelling your plans together. Bringing up an issue tactfully rather than trying to ignore it will stop you and the other person from drifting apart.

TUNE OUT
THE CRITICS

"We always go to the same places – they'll think I'm weird if I suggest something new."

Whether it's your partner or your friends, they're probably eager to try something different as well. By setting the ball rolling, you're giving them permission to come up with their own offbeat suggestions too, and experiencing new things together will create memories that you can bond over for years to come.

"I'd rather pretend a problem isn't there – I just hate conflict."

Dealing with an issue can be hard, because you care deeply about the other person's feelings and about your relationship continuing despite the problem. If you feel yourself backing away from discussing something difficult, just consider how your connection will be affected if you don't discuss it. Be brave and have the conversation you need with an open mind.

A true friend is the best possession.

BENJAMIN FRANKLIN

A STORY OF YES
DAN SAVAGE

In 1991, Dan Savage was working as a manager of a video store in Madison, Wisconsin, when a friend of his mentioned that he was moving to Seattle to start a newspaper called *The Stranger*. Dan said it needed an advice column – and he was rapidly appointed as the paper's first advice columnist.

Ever since then, Dan has contributed a weekly advice column to *The Stranger*, and in 2006, he started the Savage Lovecast, a podcast in which he answers listeners' dilemmas. In 2010, in response to the suicide of a 15-year-old boy who had been bullied for his sexual orientation, Dan founded the It Gets Better Project. In this project, adults contribute self-made videos in which they provide encouragement and support to young people in the LGBTQ+ community.

In providing a forum where people can safely ask questions about their deepest worries, where no topic is forbidden, Dan Savage has given a very powerful 'yes' to thousands (if not millions) of relationships.

Live a life
that's worth
living, one
where you do
what you want
to do, pursue
your passions.

DAN SAVAGE

YES LAB

EMBRACE THE ART
OF COMPROMISE

———

Our relationships are built on the things we have in common, but even the best friends or the most compatible partners will experience disagreements from time to time. Here are some tips to help you use those moments to strengthen your connection.

LISTEN: Instead of rushing to tell the other person all your opinions, take the time to listen to their experiences, and show in your replies that you've heard and understood what they have to say.

LOOK FOR SOLUTIONS: If we want to move forward, we need to focus on how to change things in the future rather than dwelling on what went wrong in the past. Talk about the positive steps you could both take to make things better.

SHOW YOUR APPRECIATION: When your friend or lover changes their behaviour to improve the relationship, show them that you value the effort they've made. A "thank you" or a card will demonstrate just how much you appreciate them.

BE OPEN TO CHANGE: Sometimes the solution to the problem may lie in changing something you bring to the relationship. Keep an open mind about what you can do, rather than expecting the other person to fit around your needs.

Surround yourself
with only people
who are going to lift
you up higher.

OPRAH WINFREY

YES, BUT...

Just as relationships bring us the greatest joys in life, they can also give us some of our most painful experiences. Sometimes, no matter how hard you try, relationships end in a way that can't be fixed. When this happens, look after yourself and give yourself all the time and self-care you need to heal. You don't need to turn yourself inside out to keep a friend or partner happy – but if you find yourself taking an overly rigid approach to your relationship difficulties, try to view the situation with as much openness and positivity as you can. It might be just the approach you need to get your relationship back on track.

SAY YES TO LOVING YOURSELF

6

Thanks to magazines, television and social media, we're bombarded by images of perfection all the time, and it's all too easy to compare ourselves. The next time you find yourself criticising the way you look, stop and take a breath. You wouldn't say something this mean to a friend, so how about being kinder to yourself?

We're going to look at how we can love our bodies just the way they are, enjoy what we can achieve with them and step out into the world with our own unique sense of style.

Give your body positivity the massive boost it deserves with this simple exercise. It might feel a little awkward at first, but stick with it and you'll definitely feel the benefits.

- When you have some time to yourself, stand in front of a mirror. You can be dressed or naked, whichever is most comfortable for you.

- Start by scanning yourself slowly from head to toe. Focus on each part of your body, and think about what it enables you to *do*, rather than how it looks. You may find yourself slipping into critic mode – if that happens, just turn your attention back to the exercise.

- The next stage of the activity is to look again, but this time, name the things you *love* about yourself. It could be your smile, a dimple, the curve of a hip – anything. Find five things that you like and write them down in a notebook so that you can remind yourself of them whenever you need a pep talk.

When you free up some of the brain space you were using for criticising your body, you'll have even more energy to start saying 'yes' to other interesting parts of your life.

A STORY OF YES
CELESTE BARBER

Australian comedian Celeste Barber used to send jokey photos to her sister in which she recreated the poses of famous models in their publicity shots. When she started posting these pictures on her Instagram account, the response was overwhelming, and she now has over 3 million followers. In each photo or video, Barber copies the clothes and poses of celebrities, demonstrating how ridiculous and unattainable their beauty standards are for nearly all of us – and laughing at herself and them while doing so.

Although Barber sees herself more as an entertainer than an activist, the joy and humour in her images is undeniably empowering, and a visit to her Instagram feed will always lift your mood and leave you ready to take on the day without caring about what people think of your appearance.

I've never really got anywhere on how I look... I've always worked on what's going on inside, on who I am.

CELESTE BARBER

YES LAB

GET THE
EXERCISE HABIT

As well as giving us many physical health benefits, exercise stimulates our minds, leaving us happier and more relaxed. Yet modern life makes it easy to sit still: lots of jobs require us to sit at a desk for hours and our chief sources of entertainment often involve the sofa. Most of us need to move more – the challenge is just getting round to it.

FIND YOUR WHY: We all have different motivations for exercise. Do you want to feel fitter and stronger? Do you want to take on a challenge or learn a new skill? Give this some serious thought, identify your goal and regularly remind yourself what you're aiming for.

ELIMINATE YOUR OBSTACLES: The more difficult or impractical an activity is, the less likely you are to keep it up. Aim to have as few barriers as possible between you and your exercise life. Choose a place that's easy to get to, wear exercise clothes that make you feel good, and get your kit bag ready before you go to bed, rather than when you're rushing out in the morning.

CELEBRATE YOUR ACHIEVEMENTS: Check in with yourself from time to time to see how you're doing. It's easy to forget how far you've come from that first uncoordinated Zumba class or the one-kilometre run that made you almost pass out – so take the time to give yourself a pat on the back for your achievements.

TUNE OUT
THE CRITICS

*"Exercise is difficult –
it's just not for me."*

The key is to start at the right pace and choose an activity
that sounds fun to you. If you like meeting new people,
you'll enjoy a class; if you value your alone time, a solo
activity will be more your scene. Whether you turn out
to be a walker, a dancer or a boxerciser (or something
completely different), there's a form of exercise that will
get your body moving and your mood soaring. Stay open to
trying something outside your comfort zone, but be guided
by who you are to find the path that's right for you.

"I can't go to the gym or a class –
everyone will look at me."

The truth is that everyone else is thinking
about their own performance – they really don't
care about you quite as much as you think.
Allow yourself to realise you're not actually
at the centre of everyone else's perception, and
focus on what you're doing instead of how you look.

Take care of your body. It's the only place you have to live.

JIM ROHN

YES LAB

BE YOUR OWN
STYLE GURU

We express ourselves through our clothes, and what we wear can have a powerful effect on our confidence levels. You don't have to be a fashion expert to find a style that makes you feel positive and inspired.

FOCUS ON YOUR GOALS: When you picture yourself in your new look, where are you? Are you killing it in the boardroom or shaking it up on the dancefloor? Think about your aspirations, and base your clothing decisions on these.

FIND YOUR PERFECT FIT: Buying clothes 'that will fit soon' or that are *almost* comfortable enough almost never works out in our favour. Try on a size or a shape that really feels right for you and you'll exude stylishness.

BE BOLD: It's easy to play it safe and buy the same shapes and colours again and again, but it can leave you feeling a bit flat. Give yourself permission to be playful – try on that patterned shirt you've been admiring, or those boots with the rainbow laces.

Just believe in yourself. Even if you don't, pretend that you do and, at some point, you will.

VENUS WILLIAMS

YES, BUT...

No matter how much we work out or celebrate our individual ways of presenting ourselves to the world, the truth is that we all have the occasional bad hair day. Or bad body-confidence day. Or oh-my-god-what-is-that-on-my-face day. And that's OK. Just remember that whatever you think is wrong with you is something that other people barely even notice, if they notice it at all. And those 'perfect' people out there, the ones with symmetrical, flawless bodies and faces? If you ask any of them, they'll tell you their nose is too long, their thighs too flabby, their eyebrows too uneven. Wouldn't we all be so much freer to enjoy life if we could all let go of the need to be perfect? So why not start today.

7

SAY YES
TO A HOME
THAT FEELS
LIKE HOME

Whether you live in a mansion or an apartment, there are lots of ways you can turn your home into a place that's both nurturing and refreshing. Even if you have a limited budget and limited space, you can still think big when it comes to creating your ideal space.

The ideas you'll find in this chapter will help you to free yourself from clutter, organise your life and make your home into a place to spring from, ready to take on the world with an energised 'yes'.

YES LAB

CLEAR OUT YOUR CLUTTER

It can be hard to part with our precious clutter, even though we know our homes would be calmer places to be without it. Try setting aside a day with no other commitments and give yourself permission to clear out all those things you're hanging on to that you know you'll never need again.

CLOTHING: Take a look in your wardrobe and ask yourself honestly when you last wore each item and whether you're likely to wear it again. If you find that you haven't worn half your clothes in the last year, that's a clear sign that you need to get rid of them. Consider swapping these items with friends, selling them online or giving them to a charity shop, where they can bring some good into someone else's life.

KITCHEN ITEMS: Is your kitchen a sanctuary for out-of-date spice jars and bottles of dubious liqueurs brought home from exotic locations? Do your drawers contain gadgets that you never use? If your answer to these questions is 'yes', you'll find that throwing away all those unnecessary items will make it easier for you to find the things you actually need.

PAPERWORK: Take time to go through old piles of paper, chucking out anything that's no longer relevant and filing things that need to be kept. You'll find it much easier to stay organised and to focus on your current tasks if your desk or workspace is tidy.

Some of us are hardwired for neatness and others for varying degrees of disorder. However you feel about cleaning and tidying, you'll find these tips for organising your domestic life useful.

PRIORITISE: There are a hundred different things you could do to make your home more spick and span, from taking out the trash to dusting your bookshelves. But not every task is necessary, and if you have a job and other commitments, you probably don't have time for everything anyway. Decide which tasks are critical (such as doing the washing up once a day) and which are unnecessary (such as ironing your jeans).

USE SMART STORAGE: One simple way to keep your home tidy is to have plenty of storage so that you can keep clutter out of sight. As well as cupboards and chests of drawers, consider under-bed boxes, a trunk that doubles as a coffee table, and a box to hold recharging cables so they don't trail all over the floor.

MAKE LIFE EASY FOR YOURSELF: You can streamline your life to make it easier to stay organised. For example, if you pack your clean gym kit straight into your bag, it'll be ready for your next trip and won't need to be put away first. If your vacuum cleaner is easy to get to and not buried beneath a tangle of old deck chairs, you'll be more likely to use it.

TUNE OUT
THE CRITICS

"I'm just naturally messy."

If you have to turn your house upside down just to find your passport or you regularly run out of clean socks, you'd probably find life easier and less stressful with at least a medium-sized dose of organisation once a week. Build your routine around an approach that works for you. You might like to get your weekend started with a cleaning blitz, or you may find that a 'little and often' approach is more your style.

> *"No matter how often I tidy up, my family will just turn it into chaos again - I just can't see the point."*

We've all been there. You may not be able to change your cohabitees' behaviour overnight, but one strategy is to involve them in the various processes of keeping a home ticking over, so everyone plays a role and feels proud of their achievements. You could divide up tasks between you, or turn tidying into an activity you all do together for half an hour every weekend. For your sanity, shift the responsibility away from just yourself and onto everyone who shares your space.

Good order is the foundation of all things.

EDMUND BURKE

A STORY OF YES
MARIANNE CUSATO

Marianne Cusato, a designer, author and lecturer in the field of architecture, had always been passionate about affordable housing, and when Hurricane Katrina hit the Mississippi Gulf Coast in 2005, she had an opportunity to use her skills to make a real difference to people who needed to rebuild their lives. She designed a tiny house with a floor area of just 28m², which could be built quickly but also resembled the traditional homes of the region, rather than being blank and impersonal. Her designs for a 'Katrina Cottage' inspired other architects, and soon a variety of small but homely houses were available across the hurricane-devastated region to provide homes for people who had lost everything.

Marianne's story reminds us how precious it is to have a safe and comforting place to come home to – and how important it is to say 'yes' when we have a chance to make a difference to people's lives.

One size doesn't fit all ... we're in a richer community by embracing that and creating the opportunity for everybody.

MARIANNE CUSATO

YES LAB

SMALL PIECES
OF HAPPINESS

———

If you don't have the time or funds for a complete refit, you don't need to worry: there are lots of cheap and simple ways that you can make your home a more nurturing and relaxing place to be.

BRING IN SOME HAPPY GREEN: Whether it's a spiny cactus or a window box full of herbs, adding plants to your environment will clean your air by recycling carbon dioxide and give you something beautiful to care for.

CURATE A GALLERY OF THINGS THAT MAKE YOU SMILE: Souvenirs from holidays, gifts from loved ones and photos will remind you of happy times and places. You can keep your favourites out on permanent display and mix in changing elements throughout the year to keep things fresh.

PLAY WITH LIGHTING: To avoid the wearying effects of overhead lighting, try other ways of illuminating your living space, such as fairy lights, table lamps, uplighters and daylight bulbs.

WELCOME FRIENDS INTO YOUR HOME: However small your home is, inviting friends over to share food and companionship will turn it from just a place to live into a place of happiness.

Our life is frittered away by detail. Simplify, simplify.

HENRY DAVID THOREAU

YES, BUT...

Unless we're extremely lucky (and by 'lucky', I mean 'wealthy'), we will always have limitations to creating a dream home. The cost of renting or buying a home can be so extreme that we end up living in a place that's not what we hoped for. But the idea that we'll only be able to create our ideal home in the future, when we have more time and money to renovate or move, can hold us back from making small improvements that make a big difference to where we're living now. There's usually something we can do to make our homes feel calmer and cosier, whether it's arranging our belongings in a new way, clearing out unneeded clutter or brightening up our surroundings with cheap and cheerful cushions and plants. It's easier to say 'yes' to life when your home is organised and comforting – so it's worth giving it a go.

8

SAY YES TO RESTING AND RECHARGING

Every rocket needs fuel and every factory needs a power source. We're just the same: we need to recharge fully every night if we're going to make the most of each day.

Most adults need roughly seven to nine hours of sleep daily, though it varies from person to person, and you'll have your own sense of what's right for you. It's not just at night that you can restore your energy levels: here are some ways you can integrate essential pause-and-reset moments into your day.

MORNING

Start with a stretch and drink some water.
Give yourself at least 15 minutes
(more if possible) before reaching
for your phone. Think about what you
want to achieve today.

BEDTIME

Set aside time to wind down before
going to bed, and give yourself a
regular routine so your body knows
when to shut down for the night.

DAYTIME

Get some physical movement into your day. If you can walk or cycle part of the way to work or college, you'll arrive feeling energised. Take short breaks from your work, ideally every hour. Just a stroll away from your work station will get your circulation moving again.

EVENING

Disconnect from work, and make home a place for rest and play. If you have to work, try to do it in a single burst, and then return your attention to yourself and the people close to you.

YES LAB

SWITCH OFF

————

Most of us are permanently attached to our phones. We forget how physically letting go of our gadgets can significantly reduce anxiety and allow for more meaningful, memorable moments.

You don't have to go cold turkey – it's more about finding balance, and there are lots of compelling reasons to give yourself a chance to regularly disconnect from your digital life.

FREE YOURSELF FROM NEGATIVE EMOTIONS: Seeing an endless stream of our friends' carefully curated and photo-filtered 'best bits' can make us feel like we're not matching up, so stepping back from social media is a great way to restore our sense of self-worth.

BECOME MORE CREATIVE: Swiping away at a screen turns you into a consumer, while switching off gives you a chance to become a doer and a maker instead. When you put down your screen, you'll have more time to work on your own creative projects.

LIVE YOUR OWN DREAMS: FOMO, or fear of missing out, tends to strike us when we see what everyone we know is doing. To focus on our own lives and find our purpose, it helps if we power down our devices for a while.

YES LAB

MAKE A DATE WITH MINDFULNESS

———

Distraction is a way of life for many people nowadays: we eat while we're working, update Facebook while we're watching TV and read emails on the cross-trainer at the gym.

Having our attention divided all the time can leave us feeling frazzled and disconnected from our true selves. One way to refocus our attention into a single place, becoming calmer and more able to achieve our true goals, is to practise mindfulness. The benefits of mindfulness have been proven: it helps us cope with negative emotions and pain, and it increases our creativity. You don't need to spend hours sitting cross-legged in a darkened room, though – you can use this simple breathing technique as you go about your normal day:

In a relaxed position (which could be sitting at your desk or standing at a bus stop), focus your attention on your breathing. Breathe slowly and deeply, and become aware of the air entering your body and then leaving it, giving you strength to go out into the world. If other thoughts appear in your mind, allow them to pass by without paying too much attention to them.

A STORY OF YES
ARIANNA HUFFINGTON

Arianna Huffington founded her news website *The Huffington Post* in 2005, spotting earlier than many other businesspeople how powerful the internet would become in comparison to newspapers. Her company became a huge success, but two years later, she was so overcome with exhaustion from overwork one day that she fainted onto her desk. She broke her cheekbone and needed five stitches in her right eye – it was a brutal wake-up call, letting her know that her life was severely out of balance.

Since that frightening experience, Arianna has become an advocate for sleep. She now promotes a sleep-friendly culture in her working life, and argues that it's only when we're fully rested that we'll get the ideas we need to solve the world's crises – so it's worth bearing this in mind when you're deciding whether to push on with that urgent report or to tuck yourself up in bed for the night.

When I get eight hours, I feel ready to handle anything during the day without stress.

ARIANNA HUFFINGTON

YES LAB

SLEEP WELL

———

A good night's sleep is the perfect foundation for starting the day with your 'yes' levels at their peak. These ideas will help you sleep soundly and wake feeling refreshed.

MAKE YOUR BEDROOM INTO YOUR IDEAL NEST:
You don't have to spend a fortune to make your bedroom into a prime relaxation spot. The basics are likely to include smooth, clean sheets, and curtains or blinds that keep the sunrise and streetlights out. Make your bedroom a gadget-free zone, and keep TVs, boxsets and computers in other parts of your home.

FOLLOW A CALMING ROUTINE AT BEDTIME:
Following a regular routine as you go to bed will train your mind to be ready to power down, whatever is going on in your life. Everyone's different, but the kinds of things that make an ideal soothing routine are a bath, reading a book (for fun – not for work or study), a warm, non-caffeinated drink and breathing exercises.

WRITE DOWN YOUR WORRIES: If you lie awake at night thinking about all the things you need to do, keep a notepad by your bed so you can turn the light on, write down your ideas and get them out of your head. They'll be waiting for you to deal with them in the morning, so you don't need to keep chewing over them in the small hours.

TUNE OUT
THE CRITICS

"Huh – well I only need four hours of sleep, personally."

This is highly unlikely to be true. In today's culture, going without sleep is often seen as a badge of honour, but this often leads to a frenetic 'busyness' that makes us less productive. It's not a competition, and there's no particular merit in being exhausted. Give yourself permission to get the rest you need.

"But I need my phone by my bed."

Do you? Do you really? If you're right and it's vital that people can phone you while you're asleep, at least turn off all non-essential notifications so the only thing that goes "ping" will be something that really can't wait until the morning. If you use your phone to send you to sleep (with a guided meditation app, for example), turn on flight mode to keep online connections at bay till tomorrow.

You create a good future by creating a good present.

ECKHART TOLLE

Rest is a fine medicine!

THOMAS CARLYLE

YES, BUT...

It's not always possible for us to feel as relaxed and rested as we'd like to – we all face busy times in our family lives or jobs, when it's harder to take a few moments for ourselves during the day or to switch off from technology. And no matter how healthy and calm our sleep routines are, there will sometimes be nights when we stare into the dark fretting about how tired we're going to be tomorrow (or rather, later today). But putting all the ingredients in place for a good night's sleep will certainly help to keep you grounded, and it will have a positive effect on other areas of your life, too.

SAY YES TO
CHANGING
THE WORLD

In the chapters of this book, we've looked at almost every aspect of our lives. So now it's time to step out into the world, carrying a suitcase full of 'yeses', to see what differences we can make to people and places that need our help.

If you're not sure where to start, ask yourself what makes you feel angry or concerned about the world around you – these strong emotions will point to subjects that will engage your enthusiasm over the long term.

Getting involved in campaigning for the first time can feel daunting, but nobody is born as an experienced leader or public speaker – these are skills that can be learnt and developed. What's important is to have a vision of hope for how you want things to change, and to follow that vision with patience and determination until you are able to make progress.

This chapter will help you find your voice and choose your way of improving the world.

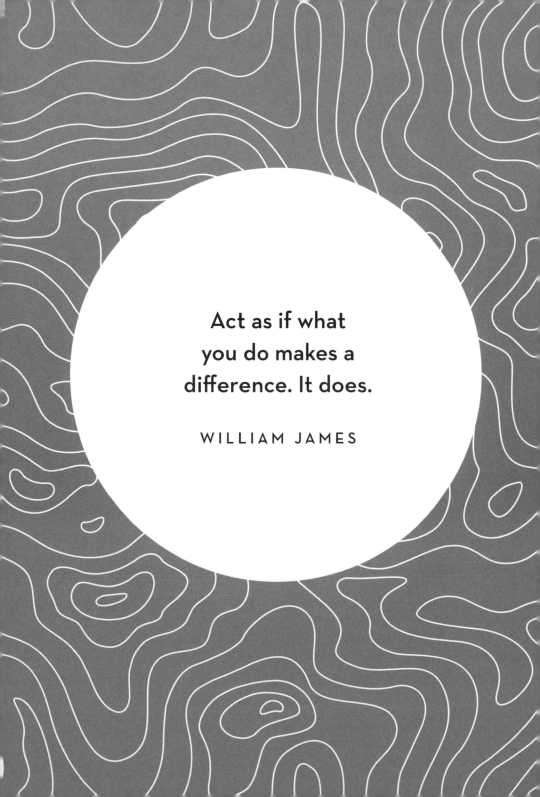

Act as if what
you do makes a
difference. It does.

WILLIAM JAMES

YES LAB

SMART SMALL

It's easy to think that each of us, as a single individual, is too small to make a positive change to the world we live in, but this isn't true. There are lots of ways we can each make a difference in our everyday lives. By starting small, you will set doable goals, and achieving them will inspire you to begin a bigger project.

Try these **random acts of kindness** to set off a chain reaction of positivity in yourself and others around you:

- Smile at a stranger
- Let another car cut in front of you at a junction
- Help someone with their heavy bags
- Ask your neighbours how they are

Look after the environment by incorporating these simple actions into your everyday routine:

- Pick up litter (even if you didn't drop it)
- Do your recycling
- Waste less food
- Walk or cycle instead of driving

Use these ideas to **help the causes you care about**:

- Give your old holiday money to charity
- Buy extra groceries for the food bank
- Take your old clothes and books to a charity shop
- Buy fairtrade products

YES LAB

TURN THOUGHTS INTO ACTIONS

———

Once you've made a start, it's time to think about the next steps you can take to get involved in the causes that are important to you. Here are some ways you can turn your principles into concrete actions.

GIVE YOUR TIME: There's perhaps nothing quite as rewarding as participating in person to help with a campaign. Whether you're joining a demonstration or volunteering with a community organisation, spending time with people who share your beliefs will energise you and make you feel deeply involved with your cause.

RAISE FUNDS: One way to help a charity is with a donation, which can often be done with a text message. But it's not all down to you: another great way to raise funds is with a sponsored activity. If parachuting or wing-walking isn't your style, consider a sponsored walk or even a read-a-thon.

RAISE AWARENESS: When people understand the issues that affect our society more deeply, they can move from superficial judgements to true empathy. Take the time to talk about the issues that matter to you with your friends, family and colleauges. You may even end up with new supporters for your work.

TUNE OUT THE CRITICS

"I'm sure they won't want me in their group – I don't know enough about campaigning."

You may not have been involved in campaigning before, but think about the skills you use every day that you can contribute. You could use your cooking ability to support the work of a local soup kitchen, or if you're an accountant, lend your knowledge to help with a charity's finances. Any good organisation will be delighted to have a new supporter, and will provide extra information and support you need to help you get fully involved with their activities.

> ### *"Everything's hopeless – what's the point in even trying?"*
>
> Achieving our biggest goals takes time and planning, and our progress can feel geologically slow at times. It's important to remember that each journey is made up of a step followed by another step, again and again. Every effective campaign you can think of started from nothing and achieved success from a series of small actions and individual voices adding to the chorus calling for change. Never doubt that progress can be made, or that you will make a difference by joining the debate.

The most common way people give up their power is by thinking they don't have any.

ALICE WALKER

YES LAB

FIND YOUR VOICE

When we start getting involved in campaigning or charity work, there often comes a point where we need to speak up about our beliefs. We could be speaking to strangers in a shopping centre on a fundraising day, or giving a talk to a group about our projects. The following tips will help you get your message across confidently and clearly.

PREPARE YOUR MATERIAL: To prepare yourself for questions the audience may have, take time to research the subject, learning some statistics to illustrate its impact if possible.

BREATHE SLOWLY AND DEEPLY: By taking slow, measured breaths, we can reverse-engineer the 'fight or flight' instinct that can kick in when we're in an unusual situation and make ourselves calm again.

TAKE UP SPACE: Remind yourself that you can do this, and then draw your body to its natural full height, with your feet slightly apart. Your confident body language will communicate to the room that you are in command of the situation.

REMEMBER THAT EVERYONE WANTS TO HEAR WHAT YOU HAVE TO SAY: People are listening to you because they want to hear your opinions and learn how they can get involved. You have a message to convey, and now is the time to send it out to a willing audience.

A STORY OF YES
EMMA WATSON

Emma Watson became famous at the age of 11, when the first of the Harry Potter films was released in 2001. As the series flourished and her fame grew, Emma took the opportunity to become a spokesperson for the causes she cared about. In 2014 she accepted the role of UN Women Goodwill Ambassador, speaking to a global audience about the need for equality between men and women as she launched her HeForShe campaign.

With a platform of several million on social media, Emma uses her network to spread her messages about social change far and wide, and she also runs a book club on Goodreads whose 200,000 members are able to discuss ideas about feminism in depth. Think about your network and where your voice is heard. How might you spread a message to promote the causes that are important to you?

I am inviting you
to step forward,
to be seen and
to ask yourself
if not me, who?
If not now, when?

_____

EMMA WATSON

Life is very short
and what we have
to do must be
done in the now.

AUDRE LORDE

YES, BUT...

Each of us has only limited reach, strength and resources – however much we want to improve the world, we have other commitments that take up our time and energy, and even working round the clock we wouldn't be able to fix everything that needs fixing. While none of us can change everything, all of us can improve something. Choosing one or two key areas to focus on and channelling your energy into them will be much more productive than trying to mend all the world's problems at once. Think about what you can do, no matter how small, and focus on making it happen.

CONCLUSION

HOW TO TAKE YES WITH YOU WHEREVER YOU GO

——————

We've come a long way since we first checked in. It's a lot to take on – but step by step, and with a positive attitude, anything is possible. Yes, *anything*.

Turn back to the exercise on pages 8–9, and take a look at your scores. How have your feelings changed now that you've reached the end? You've probably planned to put some of the Yes Labs into practice, and you may have been able to make some changes already.

To help you keep moving forward, and take your 'yes' quest to the next level, have a look at these statements. For each of the topics we've covered together, decide what you're going to do and write it on the dotted line.

Your decisions can be small or large; they can be something you can do today, or something that will take a while; they can be easy or give you butterflies of anticipation. Whatever you choose, be authentic and follow your gut instinct.

I believe I can achieve my dreams

_____

I enjoy exploring the world around me

_____

My life gives me opportunities to learn new things

_____

My career is moving forward

_____

My relationships are satisfying

_____

I am happy with who I am and how I look

_____

My home makes me feel at home

_____

After resting, I feel refreshed and ready for anything

_____

I believe I can change the world

_____

... and I'm going to ...

....

....

....

....

....

....

....

....

....

APPENDIX

YOUR VERY OWN YES KIT

———

Everyone's 'yes' levels vary from time to time. So here for your ready-reference is a list of ideas that will give you a positivity boost whenever you need it. Feel the concentrated power of these pocket-sized 'yeses'.

IF YOU WANT TO SMILE:

- Look at favourite photos of family and friends.
- Think back to that time when you cried with laughter.
- Remember when you made a friend laugh.
- Make a playlist of songs that cheer you up.

IF YOU'RE FEELING OVERWHELMED:

- Decide which part of your current project you are going to do today.
- Listen to your inner dialogue, and try changing "I can't" to "I choose to" and "I will".
- Remember that your heroes and role models struggle too.
- If you're experiencing a strong emotion, recognise that these feelings will pass and you will come out the other side again.

IF YOU'RE FEELING TENSE:

- Slow down your breathing: breathe in for a count of four and then out for a count of four.
- Spend some time in nature.
- Use an app on your phone to guide you through a mindfulness meditation.
- Go for a walk, and allow yourself to relax as you move.

IF IT'S TIME FOR SOME SERIOUS RELAXATION:

- Turn off all the beeps and alerts on your gadgets and put them away out of sight.
- Treat yourself to a pizza, a piece of cake or a fruit salad – whatever works for you.
- Have a long, luxurious bath, with plenty of bubbles.
- Curl up with a book and forget the outside world: choose a childhood favourite, a comic book, an inspiring story or an escapist fantasy.

Good luck.
Remember, you've got
this – and nothing can
hold you back when you
embrace the power
of YES!

Acknowledgements

This book would never have come to life without the positivity and support of many different people.

I'd like to thank Zara Anvari, Roly Allen and Jenny Dye of Octopus for giving me this opportunity to share my belief in the power of positivity with a wider audience.

I'd also like to thank all my friends in the writing and publishing community for their constant encouragement. There isn't space for them all here, but I'll do my best: Pete Duncan, Matt Haslum, Andy Hayward, Alison Jones, Beth Miller, Elena Nef, Justine Solomons, Laura Summers, Jo West, Francesca Zunino Harper and the all-important Pocket Friends.

Finally, nothing I've ever achieved would have been possible without the love I've received from Mary Headon, Mike Headon, James Headon and Jeremy Catlin. Thank you all from the bottom of my heart.

About the Author

Abbie Headon studied music at the University of Oxford and currently works as an editor and writer. Her books include *Poetry First Aid Kit* and *Literary First Aid Kit*, as well as titles on unicorns, grammar and seizing the day published under various pen names. She lives in Portsmouth with her husband, Jeremy. Say hello to Abbie on Twitter: @abbieheadon.